TWENTIETH-CENTURY DEVELOPMENTS IN FASHION AND COSTUME

EVERYDAY DRESS

Other books in this series include:

Military Uniforms
Carol Harris and Mike Brown

Accessories
Carol Harris and Mike Brown

Children's Costumes
Carol Harris and Mike Brown

Women's Costumes
Carol Harris and Mike Brown

Men's Costumes
Carol Harris and Mike Brown

Festivals
Ellen Galford

North American Dress
Dr. Louise Aikman

Ceremonial Costumes
Lewis Lyons

The Performing Arts
Alycen Mitchell

Rescue Services
Carol Harris and Mike Brown

Religious Costumes
Ellen Galford

TWENTIETH-CENTURY DEVELOPMENTS IN FASHION AND COSTUME

EVERYDAY DRESS

CHRIS McNAB

MASON CREST PUBLISHERS

www.masoncrest.com

Mason Crest Publishers Inc.
370 Reed Road
Broomall, PA 19008
(866) MCP-BOOK (toll free)
www.masoncrest.com

First printing 2002

1 2 3 4 5 6 7 8 9 10

Library of Congress Cataloging-in-Publication Data available

ISBN 1-59084-427-0

Printed and bound in Malaysia

Editorial and design by
Amber Books Ltd.
Bradley's Close
74–77 White Lion Street
London N1 9PF

Project Editor: Marie-Claire Muir
Designer: Zoe Mellors
Picture Research: Lisa Wren

Picture Credits:
Amber Books Ltd: 55. The Culture Archive: 45. Popperfoto: 5 (all), 8, 9, 10, 13, 15, 17, 18, 28, 29, 33, 34, 35, 37, 41, 46, 50, 51, 52, 53, 57. **Topham:** 6, 23, 25, 26, 30, 32, 36, 38, 42, 47, 49, 55, 58. **US National Archives:** 20. **TRH Pictures:** 21. **V&A Picture Library:** 11.

Cover images: **Popperfoto:** bottom left. **Topham:** background, main, and top right.

Acknowledgment:
For authenticating this book, the Publishers would like to thank
JONES NEW YORK.

Contents

Introduction

Every day we go to our closets with the same question in mind: what shall I wear today? Clothing can convey status, wealth, occupation, religion, sexual orientation, and social, political, and moral values. The clothes we wear affect how we are perceived and also reflect what image we want to project.

Fashion has always been influenced by the events, people, and places that shape society. The 20th century was a period of radical change, encompassing two world wars, suffrage, a worldwide Depression, the invention of "talkies" and the rise of Hollywood, the birth of the teenager, the global spread of television, and, later, the World Wide Web, to name just a few important developments. Politically, economically, technologically, and socially, the world was changing at a fast and furious pace. Fashion, directly influenced by all these factors, changed with them, leaving each period with its fashion icon.

The 1920s saw the flapper reign supreme, with her short dress and cropped, boyish hair. The '30s and '40s brought a wartime mindset: women entered the workforce en masse and traded their silk stockings for nylon. During the conservative 1950s—typified by twin sets and capri pants—a young Elvis Presley took the world by storm. The '60s gave us PVC, miniskirts, and mods, and in 1967, the Summer of Love spawned a new language of fashion in which bell-bottoms and tie-dyed shirts became political expressions of peace and love. In the 1980s, power and affluence became the hallmarks of a new social group, the yuppies. Designer branding led the way, and the slogan "Nothing comes between me and my Calvins" started an era of status dressing. The 1990s will be best remembered for a new fashion word introduced by the underground street and music movement of Seattle, grunge.

Twentieth-Century Developments in Fashion and Culture is a 12-volume, illustrated series that looks at changing fashions throughout this eventful century, and encourages readers to question what the clothes they wear reveal about themselves and the world they live in.

Special introduction and consultation:
JONES NEW YORK

CHAPTER 1

Offices and Customer Service

Even if people are able to select their own clothes for work, a company usually sets guidelines. In the 20th century, these have been particularly strict in offices and similar working environments.

Throughout the United States and Europe, the beginning of the 20th century heralded a new era in people's working lives. Times were changing. The

Left, a model wears a striking, modern designer suit. Right, a casual suit of the 1930s features edging in collegiate colors and a college crest over the left breast pocket.

working class began to earn more money and enjoy more leisure time. Women were entering employment in larger numbers and beginning to take up professions that men had formerly dominated. Men's employment was changing, too, with more rural workers shifting into the cities to work in **white-collar** jobs (today, only three percent of the U.S. population is employed in agriculture, forestry, fishing, and mining).

All these changes had an impact on occupational clothing. As the cities prospered and more employees entered the job market, businesses tried hard to make sure that staff looked their best when representing the company. Today's businessman or businesswoman, heading to a meeting dressed in a stylish suit and carrying a briefcase, is actually part of a costume tradition that dates back over 100 years.

THE BUSINESS SUIT

In its basic elements, the business suit has changed very little since the beginning of the 20th century. It has, however, reflected or challenged important movements in fashion.

Between 1900 and 1920, almost all working men would wear some type of suit. Pictures of road-laying gangs in turn-of-the-century America show the laborers wearing plain **corduroy** trousers, a white collarless shirt, a

Straw "boater" hats are taken from their factory in Bedfordshire, England, ready for delivery to shops. Boaters became popular in the 1930s and were worn by both men and women as casual headdress.

CONVENIENT COLLARS

One ingenious invention used by most businesspeople at the beginning of the 20th century was the detachable collar. In 1827, in Troy, New York, a housewife named Hannah Montague grew tired of having to wash her husband's shirts when only the collars and cuffs were dirty. To solve this problem, she invented the detachable collar and cuff. These were made of rigid **starched** linen or paper **celluloid** and were available in a variety of styles. When they were dirty, they were simply detached from the shirt and washed separately. The idea soon caught on, and by 1897, over 25 factories in New York were producing over eight million collars and cuffs each year. By the 1900s, Hannah Montague's inventions were being distributed across the United States by mail-order catalogs, such as Sears Roebuck and Montgomery Ward. Almost every working man in the United States wore the collars and cuffs, and such was their prevalence that a new term was coined to describe the office professional—the white-collar worker. Women's blouses were also fitted with the hard collar, although theirs featured more delicate **embroidered** decoration on the surface.

vest, a **single-breasted** jacket, and a hat—either a **boater** or a cloth cap. For those higher up the status ladder, the suit had additional features. A foreman or supervisor, although wearing the same clothes as his men, would wear a derby hat (known in Britain as the bowler hat) to signal that he was of a higher rank.

For men who worked in city jobs, the suit followed the fashions of the day more closely. Around 1910, a typical professional suit consisted of a **frock coat** with one to three buttons or a **double-breasted** jacket. At that time, fashions were becoming less formal than those of the late 1800s, so men's trousers were loose-fitting and widely flared. The usual width of a trouser leg was 22 inches (55 cm), about twice the width of a loose pair of trousers worn today. Wearing a suit for work required the correct hat. For formal business appointments, a **top hat** would be worn with the frock coat. If the company or meeting was more relaxed, then a **homburg** or simple straw boater would do the job.

IN THE OFFICE

Women and men alike received increased public education, both in the United States and abroad in the late 19th and early 20th centuries. Middle-class women in particular gained valuable qualifications and access to the explosion of jobs in teaching, nursing, and secretarial work. Secretarial jobs, in particular, were prolific, fueled by the invention of the typewriter and the telegraph. In 1900, women comprised 75 percent of typists and 29 percent of telegraphists.

Although there was no uniform for these jobs as such, a professional outfit usually consisted of a tailored coat, skirt, and blouse. A big change, however, occurred during World War I (1914–1918), a change that rippled throughout the entire world of fashion. In 1917, when the United States joined the war, over two million American servicemen crossed the Atlantic to fight. Such an enormous strain on manpower meant that women had to step in and fill many job vacancies. Furthermore, supplies of cloth for making clothes became tight. Clothes had to be produced more economically. For men, this meant that the wide-legged trousers of the 1910s were narrowed and became more fitted. For women, the changes were far more dramatic. The hemlines of skirts were raised to use less material, but the real revolution was that for the first time women started to wear trousers. This was partly the result of more women entering manufacturing jobs while the men were away at war, but also because function became more important than fashion. After the war, women's office clothing kept its focus on comfort and practicality rather than fashion, although the basic

A typist wears a typical drab office suit of the 1930s: pleated calf-length skirt, plain collarless jacket, and white blouse with a tied collar.

"uniform" of skirt, blouse, and jacket held true in most cases.

In men's clothing, the 1920s were a celebration of carefree times following war. Jackets became bulkier and were made of more colorful material, and wide trousers again made an appearance. In England, graduates from Oxford University brought in a wide trouser called Oxford bags. The width of each ankle reached an astounding 60 inches (152 cm), and although the style crossed from Europe to the United States, their impracticality for everyday wear meant that they were soon out of fashion.

By the 1930s, the basic patterns of everyday office wear were established for the next 60 years. The skirt and blouse became a standard office combination for women. Skirts in the 1930s tended to be slim-fitting, pleated, and calf-length, although some also flared out in a bell shape. The outfit was finished with either a **bolero**-style jacket or a longer suit jacket belted at the waist and featuring wide **lapels**. The double-breasted suit with extra-wide lapels became popular workwear for men, and remains so to this day. It was worn with a shirt, which now had a softer, nondetachable collar, and a handkerchief in the pocket for added decoration. The **pinstripe** pattern was especially fashionable, and dark blues and grays were typical cloth colors.

DOMESTIC SERVICE UNIFORMS IN THE 1920S

At the turn of the century, domestic service was actually in decline in the U.S. as workers found more professional positions. Nevertheless, many people still worked in private houses, especially in Europe. For women, the typical "uniform" was a cotton dress in a simple pattern, a large white apron with broad straps, and a matching white linen cap. In America, fewer domestic service employees wore the cap because it was a sign of humble employment. Often, the afternoon dress for women servants was different: a black dress and darker-colored apron. Male domestic service costume varied according to the position. A general butler or valet, or the staff of a gentleman's club, would wear dark trousers, white shirt, vest, and **tailcoat**, with either a tie or bow tie. Footmen might wear a top hat and an ankle-length jacket over their suits. Some male staff in gentlemen's clubs would dress like ships' stewards: starched white linen jacket, white shirt, bow tie, and dark trousers (usually blue).

UTILITY CLOTHING

World War II was the next big event to affect business clothing. As in World War I, measures to restrict the use of natural fibers, particularly wool and leather, were put into place. The country this hit the hardest was the United Kingdom. To conserve material, the British government introduced what was known as **utility clothing**. The government controlled the supply of material to garment manufacturers and also determined the cut of suits to conserve cloth. The number of pockets on suit jackets was restricted and cuffs on trousers were prohibited.

The restrictions hit home in the United States as well. Prior to 1941 (when the U.S. entered World War II), the zoot suit had been fashionable: a baggy suit inspired by the ones jazz musicians wore in the 1920s. With war came tighter suits that used less material. Women found that an office suit would have to serve as evening wear as well. A "convertible" suit was designed that consisted of jacket, blouse, and skirt for work, but when the jacket was removed, the suit had a more casual and stylish appearance for the evening.

POSTWAR WOMEN

When the war ended in 1945, the United States and the rest of the world returned to more indulgent everyday fashions. In the U.S., the French fashion designer Christian Dior produced the "New Look" for women. The New Look featured long skirts that flowed out from a narrow waist and high-heeled shoes. Influenced by Hollywood actresses like Rita Hayworth, who wore sweaters on-screen, women began to wear them in the office.

Since the 1950s, fashion in business wear has changed little in its basics. Today's women still wear skirt, blouse, and jacket or a stylish dress to work, while the two- or three-piece business suit is common for men. Changes have occurred along the way, however. The bowler (derby) hat, popular in Britain among civil servants and financial-district professionals, dropped out of use during the 1960s, when styles became much more informal.

Office wear of the 1960s closely followed fashion. Women wore more bright suits with over-the-knee skirts, and men wore fitted suits with narrow collars.

During this time, women's suits reflected the popularity of the miniskirt, and even the office saw hemlines creep well above the knee. During the 1970s, fashions became more informal to mirror the hippie, or Flower Power, generation. Women wore all-knitted suits of striking bright colors, and men's suit trousers were widely flared at the ankle. The concept of separates was also born. Previously, women tended to buy an integrated suit for wearing at work. In the 1970s, women began to buy color-coordinated collections of separate skirts, blouses, and jackets that would work in various combinations. This gave them more choice about what they wore to work each day.

The 1980s were a time of experimentation in fashion. In the office, women wore powerful, brightly colored suits with exaggerated padded shoulders and narrow waists, imitating the style of fashion seen in the hit TV series *Dallas* and *Dynasty*. Pants were also accepted as business wear for women, and in general, female style became more masculine. A good quality, well-cut suit became essential for men in business, and the range of acceptable colors widened to include purple, white, green, and even red.

The 1990s softened the strong lines of 1980s office wear. The large shoulders on suits went out, and instead, fashions looked back to earlier, more casual and elegant fashions. Pantsuits, however, increased in popularity, and by 1995, it was more common for women to wear these than suits based around the skirt.

THE CASUAL LOOK

The 1990s were times in which the financial ambition of the 1980s became less fashionable. To reflect this, more and more companies started to introduce a casual dress code. Instead of wearing a business suit, men would often wear slacks, shirt, and sweater. Some of the more liberated companies even let staff wear jeans. Companies that did not want to go that far allowed their staff to dress down on a particular day of the week, usually Friday.

This is how we find office fashion at the beginning of the 21st century.

Turning back to the beginning of the 20th, however, we see a different type of development for people involved in the retail and catering trades.

STORES AND CATERING

Costumes for stores and catering establishments must accomplish three things. First, it must present the right impression to customers using the service. Second, it must be in line with the business's health and hygiene policy. Finally, it must be comfortable and must not hinder employees in their work.

The "uniform" of workers in stores and catering has shifted according to time, place, and establishment. Clothes usually match the expectations and interests of the typical customer. A worker in a surf shop, for example, would most likely wear jeans and a T-shirt, whereas an employee in a quality ladies dress shop would usually be seen in a stylish suit. Some types of work, however, evolved their own particular style of dress.

Butchers and bakers are good examples. Butchers have typically been seen in aprons with vertical or horizontal stripes, and Britain's more traditional butchers still wear a straw boater hat. The hat was originally introduced to protect the butcher from blood dripping from carcasses suspended from hooks overhead. Aprons were usually blue and white, blue being the color least prone to showing stains. For slaughter men, the traditional

Butchers have traditionally donned blue-and-white striped aprons as their protective dress. They are made of durable cotton or linen to stand up to repeated washings at high temperatures.

protective clothing was an ankle-length leather apron, which was easy to clean simply by rinsing under a hose. The same style of apron is worn by today's slaughter man, although the material has changed to rubberized cloth, which is just as tough, but far less expensive.

PRACTICAL WHITE

Bakers' aprons, in contrast to butchers', were white because flour would show up on anything more colorful, but in the early part of the 20th century, even shoe-store employees wore long white aprons, which were used to cradle the customer's foot when taking measurements. Chef's "whites" have changed little since the early part of the 20th century. They are usually made of durable linen, which can be boil-washed to remove stubborn stains. On the trousers or jacket, a small loop of material at hip level holds a service cloth for handling hot dishes.

The fourth annual Waiter and Waitress Marathon begins in Buenos Aires, 2001. Most wear the traditional uniform of black trousers/skirt, white shirt/blouse, and black bow tie, which stretches back to the 19th century.

The famous tall chef's hat serves two purposes. First, it prevents hair from falling into the dishes. Second, because the hat is tall and vented at the top, the chef's head does not get too hot in the kitchen.

The growth in wealth and leisure time at the beginning of the 20th century meant that eating out became a more popular pastime. For those involved in serving food to the public, black and white was an almost universal color scheme in restaurants and cafés, seen everywhere from the United States to southern Europe. In more expensive restaurants, headwaiters or wine waiters are often distinguished from other catering staff by their full evening dress, including, for men, **cummerbund** and tailcoat.

DISTINCTIVE COLORS

Establishments that want to set themselves apart from others might put their serving staff in uniforms of other colors, and today, there is no set pattern for catering uniforms. Many modern fast-food establishments have their staff wear t-shirt, jeans, and peaked cap bearing the company logo as the standard "uniform." Some even feature serving staff mounted on roller skates. However, rules of hygiene still apply. Official U.S. health and safety regulations state that people involved with the preparation of food must wear their hair under a hair net or hat. Clothing that is heavily soiled, particularly from raw meats, must be changed—hence aprons remain the best option for protective clothing.

Dress codes for people working in stores have rarely been as severe as for those working with food. Up until the 1960s, stores tended to employ stylishly dressed assistants usually attired in suits. Department stores often had their own in-house uniform. **Commissionaires** and doormen wore brightly colored suits with long coats, sparkling **gilt** buttons, and matching top hats. By the 1960s, many of the traditions of dress for shop workers had gone, and instead, they would usually wear either stylish clothes from their own wardrobe or a uniform based on current fashions.

CHAPTER 2

Trade and Construction

Manufacturing and construction jobs are often dirty and dangerous. In the early part of the 20th century, the clothing that employees wore gave them little protection from hazards.

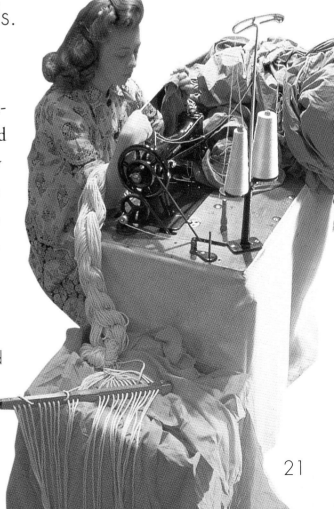

The story of everyday clothing in man-ufacturing and construction is closely tied to the development of occupational safety laws. In the United States, the period between 1900 and 1970 was one in which workers had no federal protection from the conditions they experienced at work.

Women engaged in aircraft and parachute production during World War II. The shirts and trousers (left) reflect the shift of women into male occupations.

At the turn of the 20th century, few companies had formal occupational safety laws. In Pennsylvania, the Pennsylvania Mine Safety Act (PMSA) was passed in 1864. In 1877, the state of Massachusetts passed legislation that made it obligatory for companies to put hand guards on protective machinery. The following year, labor unions made formal requests to the U.S. government for occupational health and safety laws. Yet these made slow progress. In 1900, few workers in the U.S. or elsewhere enjoyed any sort of official protection.

COMPENSATION LAWS

Improvements came in the first two decades of the new century. Perhaps the most important development was the creation of workers' compensation laws. A compensation law enables a worker to make a legal claim against his employer if the employer's disregard of safety leads to the injury of the employee. The first state to pass a workers' compensation law was Maryland in 1902. The U.S. Supreme Court, however, overturned this ruling in 1904 after pressure from industry. Yet between 1911 and 1915, 30 separate states passed compensation laws, and in 1916, the Supreme Court recognized these laws as constitutional. By 1948, all of America's states had workers' compensation laws.

During the 1950s and '60s, other laws to protect workers were introduced, particularly for those engaged in mining. In 1968, President Lyndon Johnson made an official call for federal occupational safety and health laws. Finally, in 1970, the first Occupational Safety and Health Act (OSHAct) became law under President Richard Nixon. To administer this law a new body was created, the Occupational Safety and Health Administration (OSHA). Since 1970, OSHA has monitored American employers and passed legislation to make sure that employees are properly physically protected during their time at work, which includes the clothing they wear.

BASIC WORK CLOTHES

At the beginning of the 20th century, work clothes were essentially civilian clothes, and gave minimal protection to employees in manufacturing and construction. Men working on roads, buildings, or in factories wore the same outfit—corduroy or moleskin (a mixture of linen and cotton) trousers, a cotton or **calico** shirt with durable linen collar and cuffs, and a vest. The head had no more protection than a cloth cap, although it was common for road builders to paint the tops of their caps with industrial paint to make them waterproof. Outdoor workers occasionally wore long smocks, but these had the potential to get caught in the flywheels and pistons of the new steam-powered machinery,

The miners pictured here (1926) wear the clothes that most manual laborers wore between the wars. The man in the foreground wears a cloth around his neck to keep coal dust from getting trapped in his collar.

so most workers opted for short jackets. The car industry had possibly the best occupational clothing. It had produced the first overalls, ideal for mechanical work because they prevented shirts, trousers, and buttons from getting caught in machinery when leaning over engines. Overalls soon caught on with workers in other industries.

In mining, more specialized clothing was worn. Underground workers often had leather capes to stay dry, and durable wooden-soled clogs or **hobnailed** boots. A large fantailed leather hat would protect the head and shoulders from water dripping from the coal-seamed roof. Women also worked at the mines, although primarily employed in jobs at the surface. It was one of the few industries at the turn of the century in which women were seen wearing trousers. This particularly scandalized polite society in Britain, and the female workers would occasionally wear dresses over their trousers to satisfy the critics.

DRESSING FOR DANGER

Both women and men were heavily employed in factory work, which could be among the most dangerous work of all. Women working in factories often wore their everyday clothes, including long skirts and dresses, which had the lethal capacity to get caught in fast-moving machinery. Many dresses were made of **crinoline**, a fabric that can easily catch fire and is attracted to moving metal by static electricity. However, by the 1910s, most women would wear a long linen **pinafore** over their clothes to keep them clean and away from machinery.

As we can see, items of protective clothing were few. Men working with electricity might wear leather or even rubber gloves to protect them from electric shocks. Miners wore hard leather caps to give them some head protection. Yet these were the exceptions, and lethal accidents were many. Something had to change.

The change came during World War I (1914–1918). As millions of men from Europe and the U.S. went off to fight, millions of women stepped into

Two workers fix a television mast to the Empire State Building in the 1950s. They are wearing aluminum hard hats, which were phased out in the 1960s and 1970s in favor of plastic helmets.

their positions in manufacturing and construction, particularly in the manufacture of ammunition, weaponry, vehicles, and ships. In the U.S., more than six million women entered employment, and in Britain, 700,000 women were employed in making ammunition alone by 1917. The pressures of war made concerns about fashion seem trivial, and sensible protective clothing was introduced for all. Women now wore trousers and overalls, while those in munitions factories were given rubber boots to prevent sparks. Fireproof **asbestos** overalls were issued, and workers handling dangerous chemicals were given rubber gloves and goggles. Hair was cut short to keep it out of machinery and make it more practical. Hard hats were also issued widely throughout the United States in construction jobs.

CONTINUING IMPROVEMENTS

The changes persisted after the war, especially in the U.S., after the Supreme Court passed its favorable judgments on workers' compensation laws. Many

A construction worker operates a hand saw on a wood-framed house. His only specialist clothing is a heavy utility belt supporting an electrical power pack.

workers in manufacturing and construction still wore the shirt, trousers, and vest combination, but large numbers also used army-surplus clothing left over from the war. Overalls became more common, and **dungarees** made an appearance. A typical construction worker in 1939 could be seen in dungarees, short-sleeved t-shirt, and heavy-duty leather gloves that extended up to the elbows. In the mines, hard hats fitted with lamps were standard, and miners also benefited from padded, leather knee protectors. Steelworkers donned thick leather aprons to protect them from heat and dust. Carpenters also began to hang their tools in specially designed belts, and now wore overalls to protect their clothes from dust. Steel toe-capped boots protected the feet of those in the building trade.

By the time World War II began in 1939, the big difference in occupational clothes from the beginning of the century was that people now wore clothing that suited their jobs. Fashion in the construction and manufacturing sectors was no longer important. World War II brought the same social change as World War I: women flocked into industry as men went away to war. In America, the government tried to attract more women into industry through the figure of "Rosie the Riveter." Rosie was a fictional character employed in the steel industry who was featured on posters and in advertising campaigns.

She was often depicted in overalls, wearing a welding mask and long leather protective **gauntlets**, diligently punching rivets into a sheet of plate steel. Rosie the Riveter was typical of a huge variety of working women in the U.S. during the war. In manufacturing and construction, there was no distinction between male clothing and female clothing, and the war meant that many women were no longer economically dependent on their husbands.

For the two decades following the war, occupational clothing and heavy-industry clothing stayed relatively unchanged. What revolutionized the industrial clothing market was the explosion in sophisticated textiles that occurred during the 1960s. Advanced technology was about to meet the clothing market.

HIGH-TECH WORKWEAR

Between the 1960s and 1990s, several major changes occurred in the world of manufacturing and construction. First, companies came under more legal obligations to protect their employees, particularly with the creation of OSHA in the U.S. in 1970. Second, high-tech industries, such as manufacturers of computers and advanced aeronautics, became more dominant in industry, with traditional **blue-collar** industries beginning a steady decline and with more sterile production environments arriving. Third, clothing technology was revolutionized by plastic, which was used to produce items with unheard-of strength, heat resistance, and chemical protection. All these influences came together and made employers more determined to give their employees the best in protective workwear.

In the 1960s, blends of cotton and polyester were produced for workwear and were used particularly by utility companies. These blends had several advantages: they were durable, they needed little ironing, and they were comfortable to wear. Yet in the late 1970s and '80s, studies on the safety of these materials revealed that cotton/polyester blends ignited easily, burned fast and hot, and would often melt on the skin of the unfortunate victim. Consequently, cotton/polyester blends were banned from workplaces in which the employee would come close to heat or flame.

SPECIALIZED FABRICS

More advanced materials were needed to protect workers, and these emerged during the 1980s. By the end of the 20th century, five materials in particular had transformed industrial workwear: Kevlar, Sontara, NOMEX, Tyvek, and Tychem. The industrial giant DuPont manufactures all these, and each has unique properties put into use in construction and manufacturing clothing.

Kevlar is an incredibly strong material, highly resistant to puncturing, cutting, and heat. Because of its first two characteristics, Kevlar has been heavily used in bulletproof jackets and military helmets. In industry, jobs such as glass cutting, timber harvesting, metal stamping, and steel making were made safer by Kevlar jackets, sleeves, and gloves.

Sontara clothing was actually designed to safeguard protective clothing. Overalls made of Sontara materials protect heat-resistant outfits from contamination by grease, fat, and paint—all things that would reduce the protection afforded by the thermal suit.

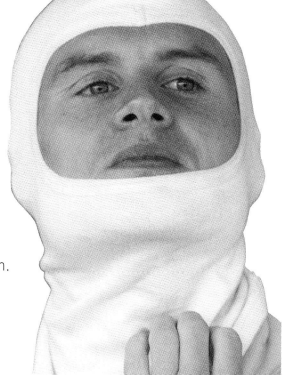

Thermal-protective suits themselves are often made of NOMEX. NOMEX is a heat-resistant material that will not melt, burn, or ignite even under the

Race car driver David Coulthard pulls on a fire-resistant NOMEX balaclava prior to a race. NOMEX clothing is used by 95 percent of race car drivers for fire protection.

28

United Nations weapons inspectors in Iraq wear chemical-protective suits featuring corrosion-resistant boots and gloves. Most chemicals suits are disposed of after each contamination.

hottest electrical and chemical fires. Apart from being used in the steel, petrochemical, and electrical industries, NOMEX also clothes firefighters and race car drivers from head to foot.

Tyvek and Tychem materials are designed to offer protection against chemical contamination. Tyvek primarily protects the wearer against dry chemical particles in the air, while Tychem protects against all chemical and biological hazards (Tychem is supplied in large quantities to the U.S. military).

Such materials gave the industrial worker at the end of the 20th century an infinitely greater level of protection than workers at the beginning of the century enjoyed. Gone were the days when the skin of female ammunition workers turned yellow from the effects of dangerous chemicals. Yet not all late 20th-century industrial clothing was designed to deal with threats of heat and chemicals. In the construction industry, employers put workers in high-visibility clothing to keep them from being hit by industrial vehicles. Garments included luminous jackets and trousers made of resilient polyurethane, which was waterproof as well as tough. Boilersuits and overalls still served as general workwear, and "donkey jackets" were produced of thick navy Melton cloth with luminous PVC patches on the shoulders and sometimes the elbows.

THE HARD HAT

In the late 19th century, a miner or construction worker might have worn nothing more than a cloth cap on his head. It was a situation that led to hundreds of deaths each year—even a small stone falling down a mine shaft was capable of killing a man. The solution was the hard hat, created initially by a San Francisco mining-equipment manufacturer called Bullard.

Bullard was founded in 1898, and in 1915, it began producing a hard hat to protect miners from falling objects. In 1919, a safety helmet nicknamed the "Hard-Boiled Hat" (steam was used in the manufacturing process) was patented and produced. It was made out of canvas hardened with glue and black paint, and featured a wide brim to protect the face and neck. In 1938, Bullard took the hard hat to the next level by manufacturing one out of aluminum, a metal that is both light and tough. However, aluminum also conducts electricity, so in 1940, Bullard produced another in fiberglass.

After World War II, hard-hat technology took off with the invention of thermoplastics in the 1950s and '60s—plastics that could be injected into a mold to form a solid, one-piece hard hat. This was the beginning of the modern yellow hard hat. Today, six million are produced each year.

Modern hard hats are made of lightweight plastics and have a suspension system inside to make them comfortable. The latest helmets feature advanced shock absorbers to give protection from even the hardest blows. Hard hats have made possibly the greatest contribution to industrial safety.

NO SWEAT

For workers in cold climates or environments, quilted jackets, trousers, and body warmers were produced. Many used the revolutionary Gore-Tex material as the outer lining. **Gore-Tex** allows drops of perspiration to evaporate out of the material, but it is completely waterproof from the outside, characteristics that are ideal for workers in heavy industry. It means their clothes do not become sweaty while they work, but they are also kept dry when out in the elements.

For workers in sensitive high-tech industries, where even a speck of dirt can cause major problems in the production line, or in chemical environments, disposable clothing was invented. These are usually thin **polypropylene** jackets, trousers, and overalls, that can be worn once and then thrown away after each use. The advantage of such clothing is that it does not build up dirt, and it does not bring chemicals from laundry powders into sterile environments.

The list of innovations in industrial clothing goes on. What happened in the 20th century was that industrial safety laws made employers responsible for the safety of their workers. In turn, the employers had to make sure that employees were dressed in proper protective clothing. Those who disregarded this left themselves vulnerable to massive lawsuits when employees were injured or killed. Thanks to modern clothing, such accidents are becoming fewer and fewer.

RISE OF PVC

The rubber scientist Waldo Semon invented polyvinyl chloride, or PVC, in the 1920s. He happened on the new material by accident, but found it to be so resilient that he could make golf balls and shoe heels out of it. PVC was soon used to make wire insulation, tubing, gaskets, and other materials. PVC is durable, cheap, flexible, and waterproof, and so it was also ideal for making outdoor clothing for the construction and manufacturing industries.

CHAPTER 3

Farming and Fishing

Farming and fishing are both physically demanding jobs. They require clothing that can protect the wearer against the worst of the elements, yet also stand up to hard use day after day.

As with manufacturing and construction, the clothing worn in farming and fishing was revolutionized by advanced new materials developed during the 1960s. Yet for much of the 20th century, farmers and fishermen wore the most basic of clothing. There were one or two items,

Left, a fisherman protects his clothes with a waterproof PVC-coated cotton bib-and-suspender overall. The PVC repels water and prevents staining. Right, a Dutch fisherman of the early 1900s wears a waterproof oilskin overall.

An English farmer, circa 1910, wears long leather gaiters over his trousers to protect them from snagging on plants and to prevent water from entering the tops of his boots.

however, that became some of the most famous and enduring everyday wear in history.

FARMING

At the end of the 19th century and beginning of the 20th, agricultural workers wore very little that could be classified as specialist farming clothing. A typical male working on the land would wear corduroy, **tweed**, or moleskin trousers (usually tied at the ankle to keep mice and insects from running up them), white shirt, suspenders (sometimes with the right side undone to allow him to wield spades and forks more easily), a vest, and a cloth cap. In wintertime, a long **smock** provided some protection against the elements. Women generally wore a long skirt protected by an equally long apron, a simple blouse, and either a woolen cap or, in summertime, a white sunbonnet that covered the neck and shoulders. Often, the skirt was hitched up above the knees to make working more convenient. A voluminous shawl provided some warmth in winter months. Both sexes wore heavy boots or clogs and a neck scarf, which was used to wipe sweat off the face or to cover the head in dusty conditions. Farm owners, as opposed to hired farm hands, would set themselves apart by wearing derby hats and a stylish jacket.

By themselves, such clothes were unsuitable for the work and so had to be adapted. For digging jobs, workers would sometimes wear an apron made of two pieces of leather with a section of board sandwiched between them. Wearing this apron allowed them to lean on their spades hour after hour without bruising their stomachs. Cloth caps were covered in paint to make them waterproof. Shepherds and farmers would sometimes rub linseed oil into their smocks to provide rain resistance. Southern European hill farmers were experts at making waterproof shields out of straw or wheat.

Agricultural clothing changed significantly with the spread of advanced agricultural machinery in the late 19th and early 20th centuries. Steam-powered threshing and harvesting machines had many exposed moving parts, and loose clothing was a definite danger. The long smocks were, therefore, discarded by many in favor of short jackets, although shepherds usually still wore smocks, and the dungarees and boilersuits used in the motor industry also became popular. Women began to wear trousers, and had to be diligent in tying their hair back and fastening it under a cap. It must be remembered that in the early 20th century, agricultural communities were some of the poorest in the Western world. In good times, most farmers would have two sets of clothing: one for working in and another for Sunday best. In 1919, the value of agricultural products in the U.S. collapsed. Farming communities were plunged into desperate poverty. When working

Two WWII "Land Girls" wear durable cotton dungarees and boilersuits. The U.S. supplied much of wartime Europe's workwear.

suits wore out, Sunday suits took their place. Photographs of farming children around this time typically show them without shoes. Farmers would live and work in the same clothes day and night.

COWBOY STYLE

Among the rural workers trying to survive this period were the cowboys—horsemen skilled in managing cattle—and in the 19th century, they were important in expanding the territories of the United States. In the 20th century, the wandering lifestyle of the traditional cowboy was over, and they settled into established ranches and farms. Yet life was still tough. Between 8 and 12 cowboys would be responsible for herding over 8,000 cattle, summer and

The rim of the cowboy hat is specifically designed to provide shade for the face and the back of the neck. It also prevents rainwater from running down the cowboy's collar.

Traditional cowboy clothing: three of the men wear sheepskin overtrousers for extra warmth during winter ranching. All of them wear neck cloths, which could be tied over the nose to prevent the rider from inhaling dust.

winter, in sun, rain, or snow. The classic costume of the cowboy was a pair of denim jeans, cowboy boots fitted with spurs, leather chaps—leggings strapped around the lower legs to protect the wearer from branches and thorns—a cotton shirt, neck scarf, and the famous wide-brimmed **Stetson** hat.

Stetson hats and cowboy boots became legendary items of dress in the United States. John B. Stetson invented the hat in 1865 in Central City, Colorado. Legend has it that Stetson came up with the idea for his hat on a hunting trip with friends. As a bet, he showed his friends how he could make a hat from a piece of hide without weaving or stitching. The resulting piece of headwear was comically large, but it gave him the idea for a practical cowboy hat. Using only 10 dollars' worth of fur-felt material—one of the lightest yet

From the 1960s on, jeans arrived in more flattering styles for women and became an international fashion item. Traditional cowboy jeans flared slightly at the bottom to allow boots to be worn beneath.

strongest natural fabrics—Stetson designed a broad-brimmed hat that shielded a rider's eyes and neck from the sun and rain. The hat was also durable enough to turn upside down and use as a water bowl—hence its nickname, "the 10-gallon hat." Stetson hats grew to such popularity that they almost defined the cowboy. Different regions of the country had subtle variations in the hat design so that other cowboys could tell where they came from. Stetson hat production continues to this day, nearly 140 years after the initial design.

Cowboy boots have an even longer history than cowboy hats. During much of the 19th century, cowboys wore almost any type of boot or shoe available. Yet in the 1860s and 1870s, a calf-length, leather, slip-on boot with a **Cuban heel**, a round or square toe, and curved top edges emerged in Kansas and Texas (there is still argument about which state invented the cowboy boot). In the 1880s, the boots were more decorated, featuring patterns of colored leather running up the side of the boot. Cowboy boots became more widespread at the turn of the 20th century, when mail-order catalogs began to supply the full range of clothing to rural markets. Cowboy boots sold for around $3 to $12, cheap enough to become standard clothing for ranchers. To support farmers, the U.S. Congress in 1896 authorized free postal delivery of goods to rural areas, and this lasted into the first few decades of the 20th century. Cowboys were more able to afford these boots because of this measure.

To this day, cowboy boots remain the best footwear for ranchers. The boots are durable and able to survive all kinds of hard work and climate. In memory of the "Wild West" days, many modern boots are highly decorated. But authentic ranchers tend to wear plainer boots, which suffer less from the tough life on the ranch.

AGRICULTURAL CLOTHING FROM 1920

The basic format of farming clothing at the beginning of the 20th century would stay in place for many decades, with surprisingly little change. What tended to occur is that individual innovations would enter the market. One of these was the rubber **Wellington boot**, which began to be used in the 1920s. Wellington boots were excellent for wearing in muddy or wet conditions, and thus by the 1950s had become almost standard wear for farmers in temperate climates. Waterproof waxed jackets, actually invented back in the 19th century, became more common as agricultural salaries rose after the years of the Depression.

The war years also had their impact on agricultural clothing. During World War II (1939–1945) in Britain, thousands of women were recruited as agricultural laborers while the menfolk were away at war. The typical outfit for a female laborer was **breeches** worn with **gaiters** and leather boots, a cloth jacket, and overalls or dungarees. Waterproof clothing was provided in the form of the **mackintosh**, a raincoat that was an important item of clothing for many agricultural workers. The mackintosh, or mac, was invented by Charles Mackintosh, a Scottish chemist, in 1823. By dissolving rubber in **coal-tar naphtha**, Mackintosh produced a flexible rubbery substance that was entirely waterproof. He then experimented with painting this substance onto wool cloth and then manufacturing clothes out of it, particularly a long overcoat. That item became known as a mackintosh.

The early macs were not ideal for use on farms because the waterproof coating was fragile, becoming sticky in hot weather and brittle in cold weather. The problem was overcome in 1839, when a new form of rubber, called vulcanized rubber, was invented. Applying this to his overcoats, Mackintosh created waterproof clothing agricultural workers would wear for more than 100 years.

The biggest leap in agricultural clothing occurred from the 1960s onward. In the last chapter, we saw how manufacturing and construction were revolutionized by the invention of new protective clothing and advanced materials. Agriculture also benefited from this clothing. Waterproof jackets and overtrousers made of materials like Gore-Tex made excellent workwear for wet-field conditions. Chemical-protective suits produced in Tyvek and Tychem protected farmers from the concentrated fertilizers and veterinary chemicals used in modern farming. Luminous polyurethane jackets made laborers visible in areas with moving vehicles.

The fact remains that farmers and agricultural laborers tend to select the most basic of clothing for the job. Farming is a dirty industry, and good-quality clothing is often avoided because it will inevitably be damaged.

FISHING

People who fish for a living have always had two basic requirements for their clothing: it has to be warm and it has to be waterproof, or at least water-resistant. The woolen sweater has provided the warmth part of this equation in the 20th century.

Wool is one of the few natural fibers that still keeps the wearer warm when wet. Consequently, it has had a long history of protecting the fishing communities of the world. In the 20th century, in both Europe and the United

A fisherman wears an Aran sweater that displays the traditional patterns of Aran. These have ancient origins, but were refined for knitwear between 1900 and 1920.

States, three styles of fisherman's sweater were popular throughout the century: Guernsey, Fair Isle, and Aran. All come from the United Kingdom, which, because of its island status, has always been especially reliant on its fishing industry. Guernsey, Fair Isle, and Aran sweaters were first knitted well before the 20th century. Such is their excellence that fishermen still wear them today.

From the 16th century on, the Guernsey sweater—named for one of the Channel Islands off the north coast of France—has been made out of the best English **worsted** wool. What makes them attractive to fishermen is that they are knitted with close stitches using tightly twisted wool. The result is a sweater that is able to withstand heavy blasts of sea spray and rain. Even the British navy adopted the Guernsey sweater, back in 1857.

The Fair Isle sweater is just as old, but comes from the opposite end of Britain—the Shetland Islands north of mainland Scotland. It is entirely seamless, which makes it harder for water to penetrate. During the weaving process, unused bits of wool are fed back into the stitch on the inside, creating a double-layer sweater that is intensely warm. Fair Isle sweaters have multicolor

A fisherman is kept dry by a set of waders. These used to be made from rubberized cloth, but now come in advanced materials, such as Neoprene and Horco-Tex.

designs that vary from white to a dark blackish brown, and can be recognized by their traditional patterns of Xs and Os.

Aran sweaters are similar to those from Fair Isle. Women from the Aran Islands—located off the west coast of Ireland—produced these sweaters for their fishermen husbands, who were exposed to driving rains and the harsh Atlantic seas. The traditional sweaters used wool that had not had its natural oils washed out, which made the sweaters more waterproof. Aran sweaters were also knitted with patterns that had local significance. Cable patterns represented safety when fishing; net patterns suggested the hope of catching many fish. Bees were another frequent pattern, representing hard work, and diamond patterns indicated wealth and success.

Fishermen still wear these sweaters—or varieties of them—today. The last two decades of the 20th century, however, saw the arrival of sophisticated thermal fleece jackets and sweaters, which have excellent heat-retaining properties, and more expensive varieties also featured totally waterproof linings. While such items have become extremely popular, sweaters will continue the centuries-old tradition of providing warmth for fishermen.

OIL-TREATED MATERIALS

At the beginning of the 20th century, the most popular form of waterproof clothing for fishermen was the oiled-leather overall. This in itself almost made an entire outfit, as it combined boots, trousers, and jacket in one. A large oiled-leather hat supplemented it. The hat's brim extended a long way down the back of the shoulders to divert rainfall away from the face. **Oilskin** jackets were also used to finish the outfit—these usually had no buttons at the front to prevent nets from becoming caught on the clothing. For lighter inland fishing, fishermen sometimes wore a mackintosh coat, but this was not as durable as the leather waterproofs.

Oilskin served the fishing communities of the world well for much of the century. During the 1960s, designers made them more comfortable by using more practical zippers and Velcro fastenings, and used lighter-weight cottons, which formed the basis of the oilskin to make them more flexible. Color schemes became brighter, and luminous fabrics offered high visibility if the wearer fell overboard. Modern oilskins are still used, yet advanced waterproof fibers such as Gore-Tex emerged in the 1970s and '80s and captured a large segment of the market.

SYNTHETIC PERFORMANCE

Gore-Tex is made out of a material called polytetrafluoroethylene (PTFE), a material that was discovered back in 1938 by the DuPont Company. In 1969, experiments with PTFE showed that it could be made into a high-performance fabric, which eventually came under the brand name Gore-Tex. Gore-Tex is extremely waterproof—soldiers have been known to sleep half-submerged in pools of water in their Gore-Tex sleeping bags and wake up completely dry. More importantly, Gore-Tex also allows droplets of perspiration from the body to pass out into the atmosphere. Such qualities mean that the wearer of Gore-Tex clothing does not become wet from sweat.

Gore-Tex and other modern brands of waterproof fabrics are used heavily in fishermen's jackets and trousers. Usually, a deep-sea fisherman or -woman in cold conditions will wear a layer of thermal underwear, a t-shirt, a thermal fleece, and then a waterproof jacket and trousers over the top. Rubber-soled boots provide adhesion on the slippery decks of the boat. Such clothing protects from the worst that the sea can throw at people.

Clothing for farming and fishing possibly takes more punishment than almost any other form of everyday dress. As we have seen, items of clothing designed hundreds of years ago are still used within these industries, and will be for many years to come. New technology, however, has given the farm laborer and fisherman the possibility of working in greater comfort and protection.

LIFE PRESERVERS

Life preservers, or personal flotation devices (PFDs), as they are known today, are items of clothing designed to make a person float in open water. In the late 19th century, life preservers were crude in the extreme. Early photographs show fishermen wearing entire vests made of cork blocks and attached by shoulder straps. Other methods used empty barrels or wooden planks. Inflatable PFDs had been designed, but these were generally unreliable. In 1852, the U.S. Congress passed legislation that required PFDs to be "furnished with ready and suitable means for secure attachment to the body of a person, or to enable persons to hold themselves securely hereto." This meant that PFDs had to be wearable, not just something to be gripped with the hands.

In the early 20th century, two new materials were introduced as alternatives to cork. One was a buoyant material called **kapok**, but this was banned after a few years because it was flammable and also less buoyant when compressed. **Balsa** wood gave a more convincing performance.

It was during World War II that inflatable life jackets came of age. The U.S. military designed them to protect submariners, sailors, and naval airmen. The

DENIM AND LEVI JEANS

Denim is probably the most widely used material in the history of work clothing. This is especially so in farming and fishing, where denim provided durable jeans, overalls, and dungarees that could be boil-washed without shrinkage or weakening. Denim is thought to have originated in Nîmes, France, in the 17th century, and it arrived in the U.S. in the late 18th century.

The denim revolution came in 1873, when the Levi Company developed a special form of seam fastening—metal riveting around joints to make the seams stronger. Combining this with blue denim material, Levi created the ultimate workwear. By the 1920s, Levi jeans were the best-selling item of workwear in the western United States. By the 1950s, they were selling all across America, and in the 1960s, Levis were fashionable clothing among the young, a trend that continues to this day.

first inflatable PFDs led to life preservers that could be inflated by gas cartridges as soon as the wearer pulled a toggle.

Solid life jackets, however, are still in use, as these are more practical for fishermen and sailors, who have to wear the jackets constantly when on deck. Modern PFDs use a special solid foam that is highly buoyant and extremely light. They are also less bulky than older life jackets. Made in fluorescent material, today's life jackets save hundreds of people each year out on the seas.

CHAPTER 4

Transportation

The invention of new means of transportation was one of the most revolutionary series of developments in the 20th century. The everyday wear of those employed in the transportation industry served to set each company apart from the rest.

At the beginning of the 20th century, horse-drawn carriages comprised a large—and bumpy—segment of public transportation. The first mass-production automobiles, courtesy of Henry Ford, were entering the market, but it would be decades before they caught on with the majority of the population. Apart from horse-drawn vehicles, **streetcars** and **cable cars** were the other main methods for getting around.

Pilots in full uniform: the rank of the pilot is signaled by the gold bands around the cuffs of the jacket. Right, flight attendant uniforms in the late 1970s reflected a desire for simplicity and sophistication.

Jump to the end of the century, and we find a completely different picture. Nonstop international air travel transported millions of people each year around the globe, cheaply and comfortably. About half the world's entire population owned a car, and in the Western world, there were about as many cars as people. Railroad networks linked almost every major town and city in the developed world.

The clothes that people wear in the transportation industry has to keep pace with these dramatic changes. Everyday clothing for these workers had to be practical, comfortable, and durable. Just as important, employees' outfits had to be professional-looking to give the public a good impression of the transportation company they were using. It is a competitive industry, and the uniform or outfit worn by the employees should give travelers a lasting impression of well-groomed style and efficiency.

CARRIAGES, STREETCARS, AND CABLE CARS

Before the automobile became widespread, it remained the job of the horse-drawn carriage to provide most public transportation. In the cities, horse cabs served the purpose that taxis serve today. Two people handled a typical cab: a driver and a baggage handler. To control the horses, both would sit on the front of the carriage, where they were completely exposed to the elements. If the weather was good, they would simply wear a good-looking suit—although breeches and gaiters were preferred to trousers, as they allowed the men to climb onto the carriage without loose material getting snagged. Headdress was either a derby hat or a top hat.

When the weather was wet, however, good waterproof clothing was needed. Long cloth overcoats would keep the men warm, while a number of oilskins or tarred capes thrown over the head, shoulders, and legs kept the men relatively dry. By the early 20th century, many coachmen were also wearing the waterproof mackintosh coat.

Alternatives to horse-drawn vehicles were the streetcar and the cable car. Thomas Davenport, a blacksmith from Brandon, Vermont, invented the first streetcar. Another American, G.F. Train, created the first practical streetcar systems in England in the 1860s. After this, they spread throughout Europe and the United States. Cable cars appeared at roughly the same time, first running on Sacramento and Clay streets in San Francisco in 1873. By the 1920s, streetcars and cable cars had replaced many horse lanes in the cities and towns, and they became the most popular method of urban transportation.

The uniform of streetcar drivers and conductors in Europe and the United States had a slightly military look. In about 1920, in both New York and

A carriage driver in modern Austria wears the traditional clothing of his trade. In cold or wet weather, this outfit would be supplemented by a long woolen coat with oilskin overgarments to provide waterproofing.

A London streetcar conductor, 1910. The logo, initials, or crest of the streetcar company are displayed on the metal jacket buttons, cap badge, and jacket collar.

London, the uniform consisted of a dark-blue, single- or double-breasted suit (drivers tended to wear double-breasted; conductors wore single-breasted), although a long, double-breasted overcoat sometimes replaced the jacket. Black leather shoes, a white shirt, blue tie, and a blue short-peak cap completed the uniform. All buttons were metal and highly polished. In the winter months, black oilskin capes or overcoats were worn. Conductors carried four items of equipment: a money pouch, a ticket-dispensing machine, a whistle, and a pencil.

CHAUFFEURED CARS

Automobiles soon challenged the dominance of streetcars and cable cars. The world's first mass-produced automobiles came from the factories of Henry Ford. Ford had designed his first experimental automobile in 1896. In 1908, he produced the Model T, which proved so successful that Ford had to devise modern methods of assembly-line production to meet demand. By 1914, over 500,000 Model Ts were on the road, and soon, other nations were following suit with their own brands of vehicle.

Automobiles introduced a new category of transportation worker: the chauffeur. For wealthier individuals, chauffeur-driven automobiles became the new status symbol. Many chauffeurs had previously been coach drivers, and so their clothing changed little, especially as many of the early automobiles had open cabs. However, it became clear that things had to change. Long coats could be uncomfortable in confined driving compartments, and top hats would be snatched off by the wind at high speeds. Eventually, chauffeurs' uniforms settled into dark blue, gray, or black double-breasted jackets, with two rows of gilt or silver buttons, matching trousers or breeches, gaiters (if wearing breeches), black leather shoes, and a peaked cap like those worn on the streetcars. A leather double-breasted overcoat and leather gauntlets provided some protection against cold weather—early vehicles did not have heating systems. In summer, the hat might have a white cover.

The appearance of chauffeurs changed little between 1920 and 1950. After this period, although there were still many examples of traditional dress, chauffeurs tended to wear standard suits and jackets. Winter clothing changed to a straightforward woolen overcoat, but as car heating systems

A typical chauffeur's livery of the 1920s. The peaked cap, dark suit, and double-breasted coat are still worn by chauffeurs today.

A London bus conductor and driver pose with their vehicle. The driver is wearing a white summer jacket with matching white cap cover, whereas the conductor is in the uniform for all seasons.

improved, this garment became unnecessary. To this day, chauffeurs' uniforms have followed the fashion in men's suits, although usually avoiding the brighter colors. Peaked caps still make an appearance, however.

BUSES

By World War I, bus travel was popular in the United States and abroad. By 1926, over 4,000 independent bus lines were running in the U.S. alone. In 1930, the Motor Transit Corporation changed its name, thus beginning the lengthy history of the Greyhound bus service (today Greyhound is the only American bus company to link the whole of the United States). Bus drivers and conductors dressed like their equivalents on streetcars. During its first 50 years, Greyhound drivers almost always wore blue suits and peaked caps, switching to more comfortable zip-up jackets as drivers made long-haul journeys. Today, the driver's uniform is a stylish blue shirt and trousers, blue tie with silver tie pin, and Greyhound logos on the shirt pockets.

RAILROAD WORKERS

The first public railway opened in England in 1823. In 1827, the first American railroad came into service—the Baltimore & Ohio line. The 1920s saw the race to cover the U.S. and Europe with rail tracks. By 1840, there were 2,800 miles (4,500 km) of track in the U.S.; by 1850, there were 9,000 miles

A fireman of the Canadian Pacific Railroad wears a traditional blue-denim uniform with the modern addition of a plastic vest featuring luminous yellow strips for high visibility.

(14,500 km); and by 1860, there were 30,000 miles (48,300 km). By 1916, an astounding 254,000 miles (409,000 km) of railroad tracks covered the country, more than the length of all the world's other railroads combined.

The expanding railroads employed thousands of drivers, conductors, engineers, chefs, waiters, administrators, and porters, to name just a few of the careers. The everyday dress of railroad workers in the 20th century changed dramatically, depending on the occupation. Good examples can be found by looking through the historical records of the Union Pacific Railroad. Union Pacific was chartered by the U.S. Congress in 1862 to build America's first transcontinental railroad line. Since then, it has become one of the largest railroad operators in the country, with 33,000 miles (53,100 km) of track concentrated in the West, Midwest, and Gulf Coast areas.

In the first decades of the 20th century, manual workers on the Union Pacific wore whatever general work clothes they possessed, usually trousers, white shirt, vest, boots, and cloth cap or wide-brimmed hat. However, by the 1930s, denim was becoming the ideal material for railroad workers. A photograph of an engineer and a fireman taken in 1938 shows them wearing blue denim shirts, blue denim overalls and dungarees, and a matching soft-peaked cap. Denim clothing became a uniform of sorts among railroad workers for the next 40 years. Dress codes have continued to be fairly informal, and today, railroad workers usually select work clothing from their own wardrobes. Increased safety legislation, however, meant that workers in the late 20th century were more likely to be seen in hard hats and luminous protective clothing.

CUSTOMER SERVICE

While manual workers and engineers on the railroads had more liberty to wear what they wanted, those dealing with customers did not have the same choice. By around 1914, almost all railroad companies had their customer-service staff in uniform. Those working in the restaurant cars wore especially formal dress.

A steward in a first-class rail carriage serves tea. Up until the 1960s, rail stewards' uniforms tended to match those of stewards on cruise liners to increase the prestige of rail travel.

A photograph of a Union Pacific **commissary** taken in 1950 shows the typical catering dress: black trousers, white shirt, and black bow tie. In more prestigious first-class restaurant cars, waiters would wear full serving attire, including starched, white linen, single- or double-breasted jackets with gilt metal buttons. Similar styles of railroad catering uniform exist to this day, and they generally follow standard restaurant uniforms.

Ticket inspectors and other onboard staff followed the styles of streetcar and cable car staff. Black or dark-blue suits with matching peaked caps were standard for most of the century, although some rail lines toward the end of the century had custom-made uniforms with more individual color schemes and features, such as zip-up jackets and baseball-style caps.

There is no doubt that wheeled transportation revolutionized the 20th century. As the century went on, vehicles became better and better in terms of performance, styling, and luxury. What remained remarkably constant were the uniforms of those who manned the vehicles of public transportation. Suit and cap still dominate among staff driving automobiles and buses.

AIRLINERS

Airline uniforms have always been at the more glamorous end of transportation clothing. The idea of air hostesses began in 1930 and was developed by a nurse from San Francisco. She recruited seven other nurses, with the idea of using them aboard the new civil airliners to give out medication to airsick fliers. They went to work for Boeing-United, and thus began the career of air hostess. Soon, all the other American airlines were taking on "Sky Girls." Shortly afterward, the idea spread across the Atlantic into Europe.

The uniform of the air hostess, or air steward, in contrast to the other transportation sectors, has always closely followed fashion. From about 1930 until just after World War II, air hostess uniforms were quite conservative in appearance. Most airlines went for tailored wool or **serge** suits consisting of a slim jacket and skirt, usually in dark blue or black, with a peaked cap. Male hosts would wear a suit and cap in the same color scheme. However, some of the earliest airlines employed stewards dressed in white uniforms similar to those worn by waiters and stewards on ships.

After the war, things began to change. More competition between airlines was emerging. Companies wanted to create distinctive images of their staff as being different from other airlines. In 1952, for example, Braniff International Airways introduced a stylish new winter uniform. It had a knee-length, blue wool gabardine skirt, a hip-length matching jacket, a white blouse, and a blue

THE HISTORY OF NECKTIES

The fashion of neckties stretches back to the 17th century. In 1660, King Louis XIV of France received a visit from a regiment of soldiers from Croatia, in southeastern Europe, which had just won a major battle against Turkey. The king noticed that the soldiers were wearing bright silk handkerchiefs around their necks. He liked the look, and so French royalty began wearing these "cravats" (derived from the term *Croat*). By the 18th century, the fashion had passed to England, and from there, to the U.S. The English nobility soon devised over 100 ways to tie the cravat. "Ties" soon became slimmer, and by the 19th century, they were as we know them today. Neckties became the standard accompaniment for any suit in the 20th century. Although their use declined in the 1960s and '70s as fashions became more informal, they returned again in the 1980s, and are still very much in fashion today.

flight cap; a navy blue handbag and navy blue shoes completed the ensemble. In the early 1960s, however, Braniff made a move away from the single-color uniform. Instead, the hostesses wore a charcoal-gray wool skirt, a white blouse, and a square-cut **Chanel**-style jacket with three-quarter-length sleeves edged in a lighter gray. The flight cap was also charcoal gray. By 1965, the Italian designer Emilio Pucci made a complete break from tradition by designing for

Braniff a bright pink wool suit, worn with a blue silk tunic, a green wool overcoat, pink shoes, and a circular plastic headdress.

DRESSING TO IMPRESS

Braniff's outfits were typical of what happened in the 1960s. As world fashion styles became less restricted, airlines started to dress to impress. In Britain, for example, British Caledonian Airways had its staff all wearing tartan uniforms and berets (*Caledonia* was the ancient Roman name for Scotland). Airlines in

The 1960s introduced bright colors and fashionable styles into air stewardess uniforms. Here, two stewardesses wear purple knee-length skirts, gray collarless blouses, and small purple flight caps.

SUCCESS OF RALPH LAUREN

Ralph Lauren has been one of the most successful American designers of the 20th century. Born in 1939, he was introduced to the world of fashion in his first job as a glove salesman. Later, he started experimenting with design, bringing out a range of neckties and scarves. However, it was in the 1960s that he started to make his reputation. He designed a series of men's outfits based around English country clothes that was a big hit. In the 1970s, he moved into design for women with clothing that reflected traditional American designs in denim, wool, and cotton. This feel for traditional American style has given him a timeless appeal, and he remains popular today.

the Far East dressed their staff in national dress to create an exotic impression. From the 1960s onward, airline uniforms have kept up with the latest fashions and have used some of the world's best designers. French designer Pierre Cardin designed uniforms for Pakistan's airline, PIA, in 1969. Ralph Lauren designed TWA's uniforms in the 1980s. From the 1980s on, air hostess uniforms became more professional in appearance and imitated business suits as commercial fliers became an increasingly valuable customer market. Male stewards tended to wear dark gray, dark blue, or black suits, and their jackets were usually double-breasted with double rows of gold or silver buttons.

By the end of the 20th century, air hostess uniforms in the U.S. and Europe have little to differentiate them except color and hat style (some airlines stick with the flight cap style, others have broad-brimmed hats). Like a lot of transportation-related costumes, air-hostess uniforms returned to the traditions of a plain but professional-looking suit as the best way to promote a stylish impression of their company.

GLOSSARY

Asbestos any of several minerals that readily separate into long flexible fibers

Balsa a tough, lightweight wood used for making models

Blue collar refers to a manual or industrial worker

Boater a flat-topped hat made of hard, closely woven straw, with a wide, circular brim

Bolero a short jacket which usually ends at the waist and is left unfastened when worn

Breeches short pants covering the hips and thighs and fitting snugly

Cable car a carriage drawn along a cable railway

Calico a plain type of cotton cloth

Celluloid a transparent plastic made from camphor and nitrocellulose

Chanel a French fashion house established in 1910, famous for its classic dress designs

Coal-tar naptha a thick and sticky black substance derived from coal

Commissary one delegated by a superior to execute a duty or an office

Commissionaire a uniformed attendant

Corduroy a durable but velvety cotton fabric that has a ribbed texture

Crinoline a fabric made of horsehair and cotton or linen

Cuban heel a heel on boots which is up to 2 inches (5 cm) high and has straight sides

Cumberland a broad waistband

Double breasted a jacket with a large section of overlapping material at the front. It usually displays two rows of buttons

Dungarees type of overall, usually made from denim, calico, or linen; a one-piece garment with straps over the shoulders

Embroidered patterns sewn onto fabric using thread

Frock coat a long woolen garment worn by sailors and agricultural workers

Gaiters a cloth or leather leg covering reaching from the instep to above the ankle or to mid-calf or knee

Gauntlet a strong glove with a long, loose wrist

Gilt overlaid with a thin covering of gold

Gore-Tex trade name for a synthetic fabric engineered to be completely wind- and waterproof, while maintaining breathability.

Hobnail a short, large-headed nail for studding shoe soles

Homburg a man's hat with a wide brim and rounded dome

Kapok a cotton-like material which was used to fill maritime life preservers

Lapel the fold of the front of a coat that is usually a continuation of the collar

Mackintosh (British) a waterproof cloak or coat

Oilskin a cotton cloth saturated with oil to make it waterproof

Pinafore a sleeveless, usually low-necked, garment fastened in the back and worn as an apron or dress

Pinstripe a pattern that consists of a very narrow stripe running through the fabric

Polypropylene any of various thermoplastic (capable of softening or fusing when heated) plastics or fibers

Serge a strong woolen fabric

Single breasted a jacket that fastens in the middle with no overlapping material and displaying a single row of buttons

Smock a light, loose garment worn especially to protect clothing while working

Starched starched clothes have been stiffened using a white substance obtained from plants, mainly potatoes and cereal crops

Stetson a broad-brimmed, high-crowned hat, such as those that worn by cowboys

Streetcar a vehicle on rails, usually operating in city streets, used primarily for transporting passangers

Tailcoat man's full-dress coat with two long tapering skirts at the back

Top hat a tall-crowned hat made of silk

Tweed a woolen cloth which has a rough surface and is made of multicolored fibers

Utility clothing designed for function, not style

Wellington boot a pull-on, knee-length, laceless boot developed in the 19th century

White collar refers to someone who works in an office or similar environment

Worsted a smooth compact yarn made from long, wool fibers

TIMELINE

1903 The first powered flight in aviation history is made by the Wright brothers at Kitty Hawk, North Carolina.

1909 Ford starts to produce the first mass-production car in history, the Model T.

1912 The cruise liner *Titanic* sinks after hitting an iceberg in the Atlantic Ocean.

1914–1918 World War I.

1917 The Russian Revolution.

1929 The U.S. financial markets crash, which sets off the Great Depression.

1933 Adolf Hitler becomes chancellor and leader of Germany.

1939–45 World War II.

1941 The U.S. enters World War II.

1948 The state of Israel is formed.

1950–52 The U.S. fights in the Korean War.

1960 John F. Kennedy becomes president of the United States.

1962 The world teeters on the edge of nuclear war during the Cuban Missile Crisis.

1963 John F. Kennedy is assassinated.

1963–75 U.S. fights in the Vietnam War.

1969 Neil Armstrong walks on the moon.

1974 U.S. President Richard Nixon resigns after the Watergate scandal.

1983 AIDS enters Western society.

1988 The Soviet Union begins a period of reform and moves away from Communism.

1989 The dismantling of the Berlin Wall.

1990–1991 The U.S. leads a massive coalition of military forces in the Gulf War.

1999 U.S. military forces go into action to prevent a humanitarian disaster in the country of Kosovo.

2002 Islamic terrorists destroy the twin towers of the World Trade Center in New York.

FURTHER INFORMATION

BOOKS

Ewing, Elizabeth. *History of 20th Century Fashion (revised edition)*. New York: Quite Specific Media Group Ltd., 2002.

Hall, Lee. *Common Threads: A Parade of American Clothing*. Boston: Bullfinch Press, 1993.

Hamley (company). *Cowboy Clothing and Gear: The Complete Hamley Catalog of 1942*. Mineola: Dover Publications, 1995.

Lehnert, Gertrude. *The Story of Fashion in the 20th Century*. Cologne, Germany: Könemann, 2000.

Polhemus, Ted. *Streetstyle*. London: Thames and Hudson, 1994.

Tortora, Phyllis (ed.). *Fairchild's Dictionary of Fashion*. New York: Fairchild Publications, 2002.

ONLINE SOURCES

"Art of the Boot" from *Texas Monthly*
www.texasmonthly.com/mag/issues/hot/2000-01-01/artoftheboot.html
Detailed history of the cowboy boot, by Tyler Beard.

Braniff Service
www.dallashistory.org/html/braniff_service.html
Traces the development of Braniff Airlines air hostess uniforms, and how the profession itself has changed.

The Costumer's Manifesto
www.costumes.org/pages/book20th.html
This site is mainly for costume designers, but it has many links and gives a good rundown of fashion history, sorted by period.

Levi Strauss
www.levistrauss.com
The history link takes you to a timeline that explains the history of the Levis brand, and denim in general.

ABOUT THE AUTHOR

Dr. Chris McNab is a writer and editor who specializes in cultural and military history. After completing a degree in Classical culture and a Ph.D. in theology and literature, Chris went on to lecture on U.S./European literature and history at the University of Wales before establishing himself as a full-time writer. His publications on the theme of costume include *Modern Military Uniforms* and *Twentieth-Century Uniforms*, while recent historical work includes essays on ancient Egyptian civilization for *The Literature of Travel and Exploration*, and editorial contributions to *Twentieth-Century Jewish Writers* and *The Encyclopedia of Censorship*. It is in the field of military history in particular that Chris has published most widely, authoring over 13 books on topics ranging from the Vietnam War to histories of small arms. Chris lives in south Wales, U.K.

INDEX